HOW TO BE BETTER AT BASKETBALL IN 21 DAYS

The Ultimate Guide to Drastically Improving Your Basketball Shooting, Passing & Dribbling Skills

By James Wilson

"When it's played the way is 'spozed to be played, basketball happens in the air; flying, floating, elevated above the floor, levitating the way oppressed peoples of this earth imagine themselves in their dreams."

- *John Edgar Wideman*

Distinguished American writer and Professor at
Brown University on America's love for basketball

DEDICATION

To my parents who raised me in a special basketball environment and taught me about life, courage, and that bouncing orange ball.

TABLE OF CONTENTS

INTRODUCTION

Oh, how far the game has come. It's crazy when you really think about it. Basketball was invented in 1891 by Dr. James Naismith to occupy a group of incorrigibles in his gym class. Then it evolved into leagues like the Eastern Basketball League (1909), the Metropolitan Basketball League (1921), the American Basketball League (1925), and eventually the National Basketball Association (NBA) in 1949. It is not just restricted to the American audience but has also secured a place in World Olympics.

In more than 125 years, basketball has gone from a single gymnasium to a mass phenomenon watched and played by millions around the world. Players such as George Mikan, "Pistol Pete" Maravich, Earl Monroe, Kareem Abdul-Jabbar, Larry Bird, Magic Johnson, Kobe Bryant, Michael Jordan, and many more, have helped popularize and evolve the game. They have left permanent marks on the sport.

Now, the time has come when you will read *How to Be Better at Basketball in 21 Days*, and you will put your own mark, whether it be big or small, on the wonderful game of basketball.

Someone who has arguably left the biggest mark on the game was Phil Jackson. He is the all-time leader of the most championships in NBA history, and the basketball coach of Michael Jordan and Kobe Bryant. He once said, *"It's not how hard you play and train that matters; it's how smart."*

Phil was absolutely right. Too often, players spend countless hours on the basketball court and in the weight room working as hard as they possibly can, yet they see little to no improvement. They simply don't have the proper guidance or are misinformed on how to fully utilize their true potential.

This book will teach you **how to become the best basketball player that you can possibly be in** a short period of time i.e. **21 days**. You will learn fundamentals, drills, and exercises that are used by top NCAA and NBA basketball players.

Whether you play for fun or play at the high school, college, or professional level, this program will benefit you. If you read everything carefully, work as hard as you possibly can every day, and stick to the program without missing any workouts, I promise you that, in 21 days, you will have the skill set, finesse, and confidence to give a very challenging time to your opponents.

You won't have much time, but you have much to accomplish, so the training is divided into three modules that are all related to each other and will help you become a much better basketball player. Before you start training, make sure you have the right approach to the game. An introductory chapter precedes your first module and is all about preparation for a successful season. There is an emphasis on the importance of **mental preparation**. The mind controls the body, thus adjusting the mindset and playing with a trouble-free mind is vitally important for a successful game.

The first module is "Understanding The Game." This chapter teaches fundamentals, techniques, and theories on how to become a better shooter, dribbler, and passer. You will also learn the tools for improving your athleticism and conditioning, preventing injuries, and recovering fully. You will discover the precise techniques professionals use:

- How to increase your basketball shooting accuracy?
- What are the most effective ways to improve your dribbling skills?
- How to improve your passing skills in basketball?

While the first module is instruction on raw techniques and fundamentals, the second module is dedicated to **drills and exercises** that are based off everything taught in the first chapter. They will specifically help you become a better dribbler, shooter, passer, and increase your athleticism.

The third module is particularly designed for **The 21 Day Program**. This module provides in-depth instructions for each day and uses all the drills and exercises that were explained in the module before. In order to participate in the program, you will need a pair of basketball shoes, a basketball, a basketball court, and a stopwatch.

Throughout the book, you will find included some interesting pictures, quotes, and some video links for reference. Moves that require illustration have been supported with pictures so you will have a better understanding of the theory.

You will be tested to your limits but, on the last day, you will notice a marked change in your playing style, your shooting will be more on the spot, and your navigation around the court will have dramatically improved.

The world of basketball is quite fascinating, and this book can make the difference between average players and seasoned professionals in a matter of 21 days!

Let us begin.

4

PREPARING FOR A SUCCESSFUL SEASON

Summer is almost over, and you do not have much time left to prepare for the coming season, so as a varsity or college player, you need to start getting into form!

What is form? You know that it has something to do with staying fit, healthy, and in good physical shape to take on the opponent mercilessly on the court, but do you know that it has a lot to do with your attitude? We touched on how the mind controls the body, so clearing your mind and adjusting your mindset are definitely important parts of the game.

This chapter deals with your **mental conditioning** at the start of a season or even before an everyday friendly game.

Knowing Your Basketball Philosophy

"I have no individual goals. We play for one reason and that's to win the title. Practice is more important than the games, and I will practice when I'm hurt, when 95 percent of the players in this league would sit out. I expect all of you to do the same thing. You will follow my lead."

– Michael Jordan

Just like your college or high school motto, every basketball team in the world is led by a philosophy that reflects the core ideas that are at the heart of its foundation. This philosophy guides your decision making and gives you the 'way forward' during your time with the team.

Remember, philosophy is not about winning. Winning is a byproduct of your team's conduct and values, an inevitable outcome of you holding true to your motto. For Chicago Bulls, under the leadership of Michael Jordan, it was **'practice makes perfect'**.

Many times, the philosophy of a team transcends the usual measures of success, such as a nice clean game or a comfortable lead on the scoreboard. Coaches of these basketball teams put great emphasis on a team game, effective communication among players, and respect. They say that a **successful basketball team is one where** the following is met:

- The agendas and intentions of all team members is the same.
- Defeat is accepted with dignity and lessons are learned from mistakes.
- Discipline is observed by everyone.
- Dedication and giving in an extra effort is observed.

Thus, the philosophy of these teams is that their team members transform into better human beings rather than the basketball monsters from the movie *Space Jam*! When that happens, everyone becomes a winner irrespective of the score.

These were just a few examples of a team's philosophy. A simple way to determine what your team's philosophy is to ask yourself: *what is the most important message I take home with me after every season?*

Mental Attitude

Determining your team's philosophy gives you and your team a head start in preparing for game day. You are more focused now but, more importantly, you are coming with the right frame of mind to start practicing for the new season.

Although the team's vision might not be very easy to grasp, there is one aspect of practice that even the slowest of people can excel at without much thinking, and that is **conditioning**. This is because your conditioning is something you have complete conscious control over. Conditioning does not depend much on funding, team morale, or management issues, and is not affected by troubles at home. While these things play a role in your life, the fact remains that the more you practice self-discipline the better you get. This is entirely up to you.

The world is a very competitive place, and no one can ignore this reality. It is no secret that everybody likes a winner. But what happens often during competitive sports is that the focus of the game spirit shifts from merits of the game to an all-out war. Fist fights, brawls among the audience, spot-fixing, and gambling are some of the consequences when sports turn into an industry.

> *"If you make every game a life-and-death thing,*
> *you're going to have problems. You'll be dead a lot"*
>
> *— Hall of Fame Coach Dean Smith*

Winning is important, but only the kind where every player feels that he or she is putting in the best effort. There is no shame in losing nor does a victory feel more deserved after a game where every player has put in 110%. Yes, we are talking about gaming ethics. When players know that they have worked hard all season, it is easier to motivate them with pep talks, they are more receptive to advice, and the team plays as a coherent whole.

Practice, hard work, honesty, and team spirit are the ingredients of a correct attitude. Most of you will not make it to the NBA, but you will know that you gave it your best. This lesson will stick with you in your professional lives, when you become an important part of a corporation or when you start an innovative business. This attitude will change your life for the better.

Visualizing Your Game

Now, maintaining focus and holding true to your conditioning and practice will go a long way to improve your game, but there is an aspect of the game that coaches often do not take into account and something that can give a significant boost to your skills; that something is known as **visualization**.

Michael Jordan once said, *"I visualized where I wanted to be, what kind of player I wanted to become. I guess I approached it with the end in mind. I knew exactly what type of player I wanted to become."*

Young Michael Jordan

Research has shown that *people who meditate and think about every aspect of the game in their heads are better prepared for the game environment* when the moment of truth arrives. This only makes sense because your mind controls your body, and practice conditions your muscles to repeat a proper movement, but the visualization gives your muscles the proper coordinates, that subtle extra push of your feet, the gentle nudge of your wrist that finally gets the ball through that net!

So what you need to do is sit in your room, with dim lights, preferably before bedtime because that's when you are most relaxed. Now, think about yourself standing at the free throw line, about to shoot the ball. Imagine the feel of the ball in your hands. Imagine the roar of the crowd, then your teammates shouting at you. Visualize seeing the ball as it leaves your hand and glides towards the net in a perfect backspin. Finally, visualize your hands in a perfect follow up. Practice this scenario in your head every day for ten minutes. Watch game plays of your team as well as professional NBA players battling on the court, so you have images stored in your head for later use.

Visualizing your goals is an important motivational skill and has much to do with the **law of attraction**. It is a very important theory to be successful in whatever endeavor you undertake in life, be it business, management, sports, counseling etc.

According to this theory, a person is a magnet that draws only what he/she desires the most. In short, *like desires like*. The idea is to expunge all negatives aspects of your game from your mind and only focus on the positive aspects of your game.

Visualize, enhance, and focus on your strengths and, eventually, they will get stronger and easily overpower all your weaknesses.

Now that you have the perfect mindset, you can focus on how to improve your game!

UNDERSTANDING
THE GAME

Before you start your first round of training let's talk about some of the mistakes that players frequently make. These four mistakes are the most common rookie mistakes that varsity players make and that even professionals overlook sometimes.

Common Mistakes
Basketball Players Make

1. **Playing competitive tournaments all year round.**

    We can understand that many of you love playing a game and drive satisfaction out of it, but competitive games during offseason, with AAU, street tournaments etc. will lower your learning curve. You should take time out for exercise, tactics, and conditioning too!

2. **Overlooking core strength.**

    Your core strength comes from the hips, abdominals, waist, and the back. To some extent, every movement in the body involves these muscles. Since basketball is a hard-hitting sport and requires stability, your hips and back should be loose and your lower back must be very strong. Weight training to improve the core shouldn't be ignored.

3. **Improving vertical by over doing plyometrics.**

Many players work on the vertical movements by concentrating very hard on Plyometrics. These exercises are very taxing for the knee, and continuous training without adequate strength can cause serious injuries.

4. **Long distance training is ideal for conditioning.**

Even though hard facts are present against long distance and marathon training for basketball, conditioning coaches and parents still focus on these methods. Let us say once and for all that aerobic activities such as this will only make you lose a ton of weight and nothing more.

Ball Handling and Dribbling

Ball handling lies at the core of your basketball game. Good ball handling means you have better control of the ball, which in turn means that you have a strong foundation to shoot, pass, or dribble.

First, become as familiar with the ball as possible. This means you have the basketball in your hands around your house, in the backyard, out in the streets, or at the school gym.

Before you begin dribbling, you must understand the **triple threat position**. It is the first thing that any basketball player should learn. Anytime someone passes you the ball, it should become your instinct to quickly put the ball into the triple threat position.

The triple threat position is when you are in a crouched, athletic, attack stance, you have a firm grip on the ball near your right or left hip (not in front of you or above your head), and your eyes are facing forward, and you are able to see everything that is happening on the basketball court. Once you are in this position, you instantly become a threat because you are able to accurately do one of three things; you can pass, shoot, or dribble – hence the name, the triple threat position.

The *triple threat position* is important because it *allows you to shoot,*

dribble, or pass, as quickly as you possibly can - before the defense can get set and be ready to guard you. Basketball is played at a quick pace (depending on where you play, there may be a shot clock), so it is important to do everything as efficiently as possible and not waste valuable time.

If you were to just stand however you wanted to, not be in an attack-ready position, and wave the ball around carelessly, then it would be easy for players to steal the ball from you. You will also slow the pace of the game by having to re-adjust yourself when you want to shoot, pass, or dribble.

Remember, whenever someone passes you the ball, it should become a habitual instinct (without thinking), to put the ball into your triple threat position!

Now that you understand the triple threat position, it is important to grasp these **quick tips about dribbling**:

o   Whenever you dribble the basketball, *touch the ball with your fingertips* and NEVER with the palm of your hand. This gives you the best possible control of the ball.

o   The correct position to dribble is knees bent and shoulder-width apart, keeping your back straight. Your *head should always be up* and eyes out in front, so you can see everything that is happening on the court. NEVER stare downwards at the ball.

o   Dribbling is always done both on your *right side or your left* but NEVER in front of you.

o   You want to *keep your hand on the ball as long as possible* (fully extend your arm on every dribble and get your hand as low to the ground as possible). If someone tries to steal the ball from you, and your hand is on the ball, you can change the direction of the ball to avoid their hands. However, as soon as you let go of the ball, it is out of your control.

o   *Protect the ball with your opposite hand*. If someone tries to reach in and steal the ball, you can block their hand away with your opposite hand.

o   *Practice with both hands!* You will need to use both hands in a real basketball game, so get comfortable using both of your hands when you practice.

Before you learn how to do crossovers, you must master ***the basic three dribbles***. These are the foundations to any good dribbler. All top NBA players have these three dribbles mastered.

The Control Dribble

The control dribble is the standard dribble. This dribble is used at slow and mid-speed. You must get a wider and lower base, crouching lower to the ground while dribbling the basketball lower to the ground. Use your body, legs, and opposite arm to shield the basketball and protect it from being stolen. Anytime you drive by someone or do a crossover, you should use your control dribble.

Speed Dribble

The speed dribble is used as you run at top speed, dribbling down the court. For this dribble, you basically throw the ball in front of you and run to catch up to it. You fully extend your arm forward and then flick your wrist down.

Power Protection Dribble

This dribble is used anytime someone gets extremely close to you. Turn your body sideways as you dribble and get low to the ground. This creates space between you and your opponent, so it is harder for them to steal the ball. The lower the dribble the harder it is for the defender to steal it, and it's easier for you to control it.

NOTE: It is important to master all of these three dribbles and be able to transition between them comfortably. For example, you should be able to run at top speed using your speed dribble, then as you reach midcourt transition into your control dribble, then transition into your power protection dribble if your defender gets too close to you.

SITUATION: **Someone passes you the ball.**
You catch it and immediately put it into your triple threat.
Now, you want to get around your defender. How do you do it?

ANSWER: When you are in your triple threat position,
there are two basic ways to get around someone without
simply dribbling and then going into a crossover. You should
attempt to use these moves before doing any crossovers.

The first way is *the basic rip through drive*. You rip the ball in front of you and off to the side a bit, as you drive by your opponent. You must make sure you rip the ball low to the ground, so it will be difficult for your defender to steal. You must drive in a straight line, as much as possible, and try to blow by your defender.

The second way is *the jab fake, rip through drive*. This is the same as the rip through drive, except you fake going in one direction, then you go the other way. The key to this is really making it look as if you are going to go in one direction, then go the other way. You can make it look as if you are going in the direction by jabbing quickly with your foot and entire body, and by faking with the ball. Make sure you dribble the ball on the ground before you lift your pivot foot off the ground, otherwise you will receive a call for traveling.

Crossovers

Now that you understand how to get the ball into the triple threat position and drive off the dribble, it is important to know **how to do a crossover**. What is a crossover? *A crossover is when you are dribbling the basketball in one hand and you fake like you are going to go in one direction, then you quickly switch the ball to the other hand and go in the opposite direction.* Read these **crossover tips** before you get started!

- In order to do a good crossover, you have to really sell the fake. Your opponent has to really believe that you are going to go in the direction that you want him to think you are going in. How do you do this? The simplest way to do this is to practice and literally make your crossovers look identical to what you would do if you were actually going in that direction. This may be hard at first, but, with enough practice, it will become effortless.

- Moving the ball as quickly as you can is essential to a good crossover. You must do every crossover extremely quickly, so your defender will have a hard time reacting and cutting you off. No matter how quick your running and explosive speed is, if you can't do a quick enough crossover to keep up, you will have problems.

- Keep your head up so you can see what is happening around you on the basketball court and use your opposite hand to protect the ball from your defender reaching in.

- Go in a straight line. The quickest way from point A to point B is in a straight line. When you try to go around your defenders, attack them at straight-on angles. Don't run in a curve and try to get around them.

- Always be in control!

These are **the basic four-and-a-half fundamental crossovers** that are used in basketball. Each crossover has a specific time that it should be used. Any other double or triple crossovers are based off using these four-and-a-half crossovers. *Master these four-and-a-half crossovers and you will become a master of dribbling.*

1. ***The basic left-to-right, or right-to-left crossover.*** This is simply dribbling with one hand and then switching to the other. It's simple but extremely effective. It should be used whenever you have enough space between you and your defender so that they cannot steal the ball.

2. ***The between-the-legs crossover.*** This crossover should be used when you are closer to your defender, and the ball would get stolen if you were to use a regular left to right/right to left crossover.

3. ***The behind-the-back crossover.*** This crossover should be used when your defender is extremely close to you. You do not have enough space to do a regular crossover or between the legs crossover.

4.   ***The spin crossover.*** This should be used when the defender is extremely close to you and they are already leaning a bit in one direction. Whatever way they are leaning, you simply do a spin and rotate around them in the opposite direction.

5.   ***The half crossover,*** the in and out. This is a good crossover to use when you want to fake using a screen and go in the opposite direction. It is also a great setup for a double crossover but can be used at any time to get around someone (if there is enough space).

Double and triple crossovers are used if your defender cuts you off after you have done your first crossover. If this happens, you simply do another crossover (double crossover), and if you get cut off one more time, you do another crossover (triple crossover). Double and triple crossovers consist of any combinations of the four-and-a-half fundamental crossovers.

Shooting

Offense wins matches, and at the core of every offense lies good shooters. If you analyze some of the greatest shooters of all time, from Reggie Miller to Ray Allen, to Michael Jordan, you will notice that all of them shoot the basketball with a different technique, yet, they are all great shooters. Therefore, it is not about what technique you use to shoot the basketball, but what qualities your technique allows you to have. If your basketball shooting technique allows you to have these three qualities, you will instantly be a great shooter.

1. *Fast Release.* If you can't release the ball fast enough, players will block your shot. Therefore, you need to be able to release the ball as quickly as you can to avoid players from contesting or blocking your shot.

2. *Accuracy.* This is plain and simple. You need to be able to accurately shoot the ball and get it in. Whether it is to bank the shot off the backboard, or simply shoot the ball in the net, you need accuracy.

3. *Consistency.* You need to be able to consistently get the ball in the net. This is achieved by shooting with the same technique every time.

If your technique allows you to have these three qualities, it doesn't matter if your shot looks ugly or pretty, ***you will be a great shooter.*** Think about it, if you can shoot the ball so quickly that no one can block you, and you consistently get the ball in every time, how are you not a great shooter?

That being said, there is a general technique that nearly every single high school, NCAA, and NBA player uses, that allows them to shoot the ball accurately, consistently, and fast.

You are about to learn the **basketball shooting technique** that has been passed down from generation to generation and **used by many NBA players**. However, take into consideration, if you are trying to emulate a professional, that even if you are using the identical technique, everyone's shot will look different because of their height, body weight, limb lengths, and proportions. That being said, just because your shot may not look exactly like Michael Jordan's or Ray Allen's, it doesn't mean that you aren't a great shooter!

When you are learning your basketball shooting technique, always remember what you want your technique to produce – a fast release, accuracy, and consistency.

Step 1: Shooting Stance

Get into your triple threat position, face your feet and body to the net, make sure your torso is completely upright (not leaning in any direction), and stare at the rim. It doesn't matter if you stare at the front, back, or entire rim. Every player is different. Choose whatever you feel comfortable doing and stick to it!

Your feet should be about shoulder-width apart, however, some people may have a wider or narrower distance between their feet, depending on personal preference. The important thing is to be in a comfortable position where you are balanced and able to comfortably jump and shoot. Many right-handed NBA players prefer to have their right foot slightly ahead of their left foot, and left-handed players prefer to have their left foot slightly ahead of their right. The stronger leg will take charge of your jump.

Your torso should be in a completely upright position. In other words, you don't want to lean too far forward, backward, or to the side. This is one quality that Ray Allen has that separates him from other players. His torso stays completely upright throughout his entire shot.

It doesn't matter what type of shot you are shooting (3-point, free throw, shooting off screen, step back, pull up), before you leave the ground, you should be in your triple threat position, your body and feet should face the net, your eyes should be focused on the rim, and your torso should be upright and balanced.

Step 2: Holding the Ball

NOTE: You are currently in your triple threat position with your feet and body facing the net, your eyes are focused on the rim, and your torso is upright and balanced.

First, spread your fingertips so they cover a comfortable amount of the ball. REMEMBER: *The ball should be* **on your fingertips** *and not touching your palm.* This allows for optimum control.

Second, your shooting hand is your dominant hand and should be placed in the middle of the ball, and your guide hand should be placed on the side. REMEMBER: *You do not actually shoot the ball with your guide hand.* It is only used to hold onto the ball and help aim or "guide" the shot.

Third, your *fingertips should be lined up perpendicular to the seams of the basketball.* This allows the ball to get a perfect backspin upon release, which will help increase its trajectory and also increase its chances of going in if it bounces off the rim. However, even the best NBA players don't always line their fingers up perpendicular to the seams. If the shot clock is running down, or someone is close to them and they do not have enough time, they will just shoot the ball however it is resting in their hands. Don't ever line your fingers up perpendicular to the seams if it means sacrificing a fast release and puts you in jeopardy of getting blocked.

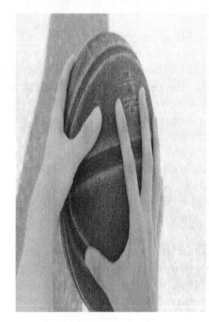 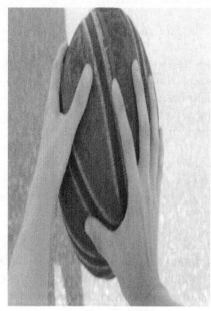

RIGHT   WRONG

Step 3: The Two 90-Degree Hooks

NOTE: You are currently in your triple threat position with your feet and body facing the net, your eyes are focused on the rim, your torso is upright and balanced, your shooting hand is spread out in the middle of the ball (lined up perpendicular to the seams if you have enough time), and your guide hand is spread out on the side of the ball.

Next, you need to create two 90-degree hooks.

First, you need to bend your wrist backward until it goes to roughly 90 degrees; this is **the first 90-degree hook.**

Second, bend your forearm backward, until the point where your forearm and bicep meet and create roughly a 90-degree angle. ***This is the second 90-degree hook.***

So at this point, you should have two 90-degree hooks, one at your wrist, and one in your arm. You should create these hooks before you even begin to rise up and shoot. This will set you up for a fast release.

Step 4: Rising Up

NOTE: *You are still in your triple threat position with your feet and body facing the net, your eyes are focused on the rim, your torso is upright and balanced, your shooting hand is spread out in the middle of the ball (lined up perpendicular to the seams if you have enough time), your guide hand is spread out on the side of the ball, and you have created two 90-degree hooks with your hand and arm.*

You will now raise the ball up toward your head as you simultaneously begin to jump.

Maintain the torso in its upright position. You will bring the ball up in a completely straight line from your feet all the way up to your head. Your shooting elbow should be under the ball and in alignment with your foot, knee, and hip.

You will maintain the two 90-degree hooks the entire time as you bring the ball toward your head and begin your jump. Just before your feet leave the ground and the ball is near the top of your head, you will reach your *set point*. This is the point that you stop at before you extend your arm and flick your wrist to shoot. You will actually stay in your set point for a fraction of a second until you reach the top of your jump and release your shot. Every player has a different set point. Someone like Kevin Garnett's set point is actually behind his head. However, the majority of NBA players' set points are slightly above their head and in front of their face. Play around and find a comfortable set point and stick to it!

Step 5: Leaving the Ground and Releasing the Shot

NOTE: You are now at your set point and about to leave the ground, rising up through the air.

Your feet and body will now leave the ground and you will rise into the air. You keep the ball and your entire body in the exact same position that it was in before you left the ground until you are near the top of your jump. Do not lean in any direction.

Once you are near the top of your jump, extend your arm upward into the air and flick your wrist downward as you keep your fingertips spread, and the ball leaves your hands toward the net. Your fingers should end up like a fish hook, pointing toward the ground. Time your shot so that the ball leaves your hands when you are at the top of your jump (highest point in the air).

The TV show *Sports Science* calculated that the optimum angle of release that your arm should be at when you shoot is 46 to 50 degrees. After the ball leaves your hands, many top coaches teach their players to hold their release. This means that you maintain the same position that you had when the ball left your hands. This allows you to get a good follow through and enables you to analyze your shot. For example, you can look at your arm/wrist/fingers and see if the angle of your arm was too high/low/far to the right/far to the left, and to see if your wrist was bent down enough and your fingers were spread out enough.

Step 6: Analyzing the Shot

The ball has left your hands and it will have done one of two things; go in or miss. No matter what happens, every time, after you shoot, analyze what happened. Think about what you did wrong and what you did right. Learn from any mistakes you made and make the proper adjustments for the next shot you take.

TIP: Get a video camera and record yourself shooting. By doing this, you will pick up on many details that you wouldn't have noticed from shooting without a camera. Sometimes you think your body is doing one thing, but it is actually doing something completely different. A camera can save you a lot of time when learning how to shoot properly. Many top NCAA and NBA players have analyzed videos of their shots at some point or another in their careers.

Taking the Free Throw Shot

Now, a free shot may look like it is the easiest shot of the game because there is no defense. But the absence of defense is the very reason the shot is so difficult. When you stand on the free shot line, all eyes are on you, and you have to meet the expectations of your teammates and the audience, and you feel the true power of the game, which is very different from practice. But here is what *Michael Jordan* says is the **right way for free throw shooting**:

1. Make sure you have your balance. It does not mean that both of your feet must be parallel. Some players keep their right foot or the left foot slightly ahead to maintain proper balance.

2. As you get into balance, you must clear your mind of the game and think about your practice sessions. That way, you will be relaxed and comfortable. This is very important.

3. Once you have the balance, you have three choices for focal points, i.e. your target: the rim, inside the rim or the back of the rim.

4. When you raise your hand, the ball must be at your fingertips, while your forearm should be vertical. The ball should not be on your palms since that will lessen your control over the ball.

5. When taking the shot, try to force your first three fingers from the thumb to work more than the last two. This will create backspin and increase the possibility of the ball going in the basket if it hits the rim.

6. While shooting, the force must come from your feet, transfer through the rest of your body, and release through your fingers as you take the shot.

7. Lastly, make free shooting a ritual and only use the same set of movements every time you take a shot. For Michael Jordan, it was spinning the ball once, dribbling it three times, and spinning it again right before taking the shot.

Mastering Long Range Shooting

The coveted 3-point shot is considered the epitome of basketball shots. Taking the shot on the game bell and making a perfect 'swish' with the ball is a finale akin to a boxing knockout win. Let's look at some ***advanced basketball shooting tips***:

Eyes on the Rim!

Shouldn't the title say eye on the *ball*? Well, no. The aim of dribbling and ball handling exercise is to get as much eye time away from the ball as possible. You should focus on anything but the ball, and the more you practice the less frequent you will need to look at the ball.

Instead, as a shooter, you must keep your attention on the rim. Always know exactly where the rim is because then your brain subconsciously keeps the angle and distance calculation. This increases your focus and increases the chance of making the basket when you actually shoot.

Proper Finish

After you have taken the shot, it is very important to have the correct follow through. Your wrist should be relaxed and not tense. The entire motion from the shooting to follow up should be one fluid movement.

Before the start of each game or practice, try shooting 50 shots from the free throw line to get the feel of a shot.

Do Not Try to Shoot Like Kobe Bryant

Kobe Bryant is not an ordinary basketball player. He is an all-star player who lives and breathes basketball with thousands of hours of practice under his belt. Do not mimic him and stick with the basics. Shoot as you are going up and release the ball at the top of your jump.

Avoid Thinking about Your Shot

Never think about shot mechanics during the game. A game is not the time to analyze your skill or technique. Just like a final exam you should be more concerned about winning the game and scoring rather than tip and technique. That is done during practice.

If you want to think, think that it doesn't matter if you make the basket. If it does make the basket, congratulate yourself and move on. If it does not, tell yourself that it was a nice try and you will make it next time.

Tips like these are important for your game psyche and natural form.

Practicing of Shooting Drills

Instead of standing, waiting to shoot hoops, try to restrict shooting the ball to only after an exhaustive drill. This will test how well you perform in the middle of the game. In fact, this is the only way shooting drills should be practiced during a practice.

Passing

Basketball is a team game. All of the five players should work as cogs in a wheel, each relying on one another for support, while making sure they do their part most efficiently.

Your team strength may not lie in shooting killer hoops or blocking impossible ones from the opposite side, but, if you have good coordination and trust among each other, your ball possession will increase many folds and, hence, the chances of scoring.

And yet, we see passing as a very under-taught aspect of the sport. Passing has been reduced to a matter of necessity only when a player does not see an opening for a shot. This attitude will not do, and you need to work hard to improve coordination, skill, trust, and ball handling to make your team a disciplined family.

Just like shooting, it is not necessarily about how good your technique is, but what qualities your passing technique allows you to have. Your passes should be **accurate, fast, and consistent**. You should be able to pass the ball accurately to your teammates' hands, pass the ball fast enough to them so that no one will steal the ball, and do this consistently - every single time.

Main Types of Passes

The **chest pass** is made from the chest and is the most common pass in basketball. To make a chest pass, place your thumbs near the back of the ball, and then, extend your arms forward and snap your thumbs down (towards the ground), and face your palms outwards. The ball should be thrown at the receiver's chest.

The **bounce pass** uses the exact same technique as the chest pass, however, you bounce the ball against the floor first, to sneak the ball between defenders' arms. You should bounce the ball two-thirds of the way between yourself and your teammate. If you bounce the ball closer than this, the ball will slow down and float in the air for a long time, making it easy for the defender to steal. A bounce pass should reach the player in a single bounce at about waist height.

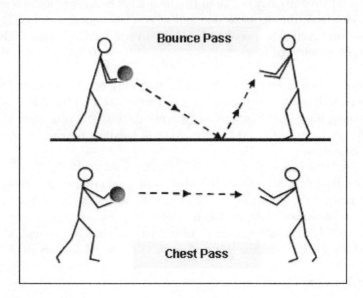

The **overhead pass** uses the exact same technique as the chest pass, however, you do it from over the top of your head. Your fingers still end up pointing toward the ground with your palms facing outwards. This pass is used when you need to pass to defenders far away from you or skip the pass across the three-point line, over defenders' heads, to your teammates. Aim for the receiver's chin and don't take the ball behind your head.

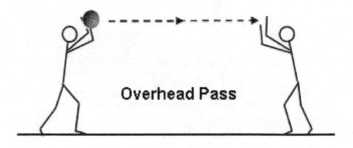

The **dribble pass** is used to quickly transfer the ball with one hand to a nearby teammate while dribbling. This move takes practice to master. Steve Nash is often seen practicing this move.

The **baseball pass** is made when the ball has to travel an extremely long distance. You throw the ball just like you would throw a baseball. This is an advance pass, and rigorous practice is required before using it.

Defense

All coaches have different theories on how to play defense. Therefore, it becomes difficult and almost pointless to give you specific assignments on how to guard someone. We could tell you one thing, and your coach tells you another.

Some coaches tell you to force the player you are guarding to the outside of the court; other coaches say to the middle of the court. Some coaches want you to defend a player close; other coaches want you to sag off the player. Some coaches want you to play your man full court on defense; other coaches want you to pick them up at half court. Some coaches play man defense; other coaches play zone. Some coaches want you to help out your teammates if they get beat on defense; other coaches tell you never to leave the player you are guarding.

In general, each coach has their own theory, and there are endless different assignments that a coach can give a player. Therefore, we will explain the basic principles and techniques that will allow you to **play optimal defense** and **properly execute whatever assignment your coach gives you**!

Defensive Stance

The first thing to learn is the proper defensive stance. While maintaining a defensive stance, balance is key. Anyone can stand with arms spread out, but few have the right balance to provide formidable resistance. Here are the key features of a defensive basketball position:

- Your feet must be spread out wider than shoulder width since that will provide your body a firm base.
- Your weight must be borne by the balls of your feet, but the heels must be in contact with the ground at all times.
- Your back should be as straight as possible, so you have the strength of the back in your stance as well.
- Knees should be bent slightly inwards and in a half squat position for greater push power.
- Your torso should be leaning forward slightly, and your arms should be spread wide apart.

The Defensive Slide

Whenever you move left to right, **your feet should never cross over each other**! Instead, point your lead foot in the direction you are going in (if you are moving left, then your left foot is your lead foot and vice versa), and then lift your lead off the ground and push yourself (slide) by using force from your other leg.

The Defensive Change of Direction

Whenever your defender changes directions, you must also. You do this by planting your outside foot, and then pivoting and changing directions. You want to make the plant and pivot as quickly as possible.

Boxing Out

Whenever someone shoots the ball, do NOT chase after it. Instead, find the player you are defending, place your forearm on them so they can't get around you, and then pivot around and jam your butt into their leg. This will stop them from getting the ball. This is called boxing out and all coaches expect their players to do this instead of just chasing the ball. If everyone on the team boxes out their defenders, it increases their chances of getting the rebound.

Middle of the Court Rule

Never let the opponent play you from the center of the court. Always force him to the left wing or the right wing. The reason is simple; taking a shot from the center has a higher success percentage than taking it from an angle.

So, when you are playing man to man, always stand at an angle so your opponent finds it harder to sneak to the center.

Blocking with the Elbows

As you block the player, you must block him with arms raised and elbows behind you, unlike when you face an opponent with the ball where you spread your arms wide behind you. This enables you to block the opponent with your forearm and makes it difficult for him to tackle and come forward.

General Tips

Although most coaches have their own theories and principles, nearly all coaches expect the following from a defender:

- Get your hand up to contest every shot.
- Try your best to keep your defender in front of you (not let them get around you).
- Box out all the time.
- Put in your best effort.

DEFENSIVE CONCLUSION: If you follow all these techniques and principles, and then follow whatever instructions your coach gives you, you will be an ultimate defender!

Athleticism

No matter how good your technique and skills are, if you face a more athletic player than yourself, you are going to have some troubles. ***Being able to jump high, run quickly, and have sufficient strength is extremely important when it comes to being a great basketball player.*** Luckily, all of these qualities can be improved.

The main exercises that are used to improve your strength, vertical jump, and speed, go hand in hand; what improves one, will also improve another.

First, we're going to explain how to jump higher and run quicker. Strength will tie in with these topics!

How Do I Jumper Higher and Run Quicker?

There are well-known general principles that have helped many people enhance their vertical jumps, run faster, and turn into top athletes. College and professional players alike have employed these principles. Following them can work for increasing your vertical jump and speed, as well!

If you think about physics, you can unlock the secret to jumping and running faster. Improving the height of a vertical jump and rate of speed comes down to this simple idea: **Increasing your power-to-body weight ratio**. Doing this, as per science-based results, will enhance your vertical jump and rate of speed.

How Do I Gain More Power?

In physics, *Power* is determined by multiplying the rate of Force by the rate of Velocity.

We will define *force* as a person's maximum amount of **strength** and *velocity* as a person's maximum amount of **speed**. Based on the above formula, increasing max strength and max velocity (in proportion to your body weight) will improve the power of your vertical jump and speed. This simple principle has helped many top athletes!

How Do I Gain More Strength?

There is an effective way to measure strength in terms of enhancing your vertical jump and speed. How well are you performing exercises such as the *full Olympic back squat, front squat, powerlifting-style squat, box squat,* and *deadlift?*

If you can **increase the amount of weight you lift while doing these exercises**, in proportion to your body weight, the height of your vertical jump and rate of speed will increase.

NOTE: How to do these exercises will be explained under **Drills and Exercises**.

How Do I Gain More Velocity?

We will define *velocity* in terms of the speed of your approach to the vertical jump and the speed of your strides when running. The average vertical jump happens in about .2 seconds. Enhanced velocity reflects your overall strength, and an effective way to increase velocity is in mastering exercises like *depth jumps, shock jumps, broad jumps, jumping,* and *sprinting*.

NOTE: How to do these exercises will be explained under **Drills and Exercises**.

The following examples will help you understand these principles.

First Example:

Athlete #1: Body weight 150 lbs., Max. Squat 300 lbs., Max. Power in Vertical Jump 275 lbs.

Athlete #2: Body weight 150 lbs., Max. Squat 300 lbs., Max. Power in Vertical Jump 150 lbs.

Both athletes carry the same body weight and have the same max squat, however, it's in the power of the vertical jump where they differ. Athlete #1 exerts 275 lbs. of force, while Athlete #2 exerts only 150 lbs. This inherent difference determines that **Athlete #1 will jump higher**. Athlete #2 needs to boost his velocity so his strength will carry over into the vertical jump.

Second Example:

Athlete #1: Body weight 150 lbs., Max. Squat 300 lbs., Max. Power in Vertical Jump 290 lbs.

Athlete #2: Body weight 250 lbs., Max. Squat 300 lbs., Max. Power in Vertical Jump 290 lbs.

Both athletes have the same max squat and exert the same max power in their vertical jumps, however, Athlete #1 is 100 pounds lighter. This determines that **Athlete 1** has a better ratio of overall power to body weight and **will leap higher**. Athlete #2 would have to cut body weight to gain similar height.

Third Example:

Athlete #1: Body weight 150 lbs., Max. Squat 150 lbs., Max. Power in Vertical Jump 150 lbs.

Athlete #2: Body weight 150 lbs., Max. Squat 400 lbs., Max. Power in Vertical Jump 375 lbs.

Both athletes have the same body weight, but Athlete #2 outperforms with a max squat that is 250 pounds greater and max power in the vertical jump that is 225 pounds greater. It must be clear that **Athlete #2 will jump much higher**, because there is much more strength, even for having the same body weight. Most of that strength will be displayed in the quick velocity of the vertical jump. Athlete #1 could improve their vertical jump by increasing the max squat, which could enhance velocity by increasing leg strength.

Besides having leg strength, it is also important to develop strength in the upper body. Exercises like the *bench press*, *pull ups*, *chin ups*, *military press*, and *barbell rows* help increase your upper body strength.

NOTE: How to do these exercises will be explained under ***Drills and Exercises***.

Conditioning

Being able to run up and down the court without getting tired is essential to being a great basketball player. If you get too tired when you are playing, you won't be able to think properly or execute any of the movements that you have to.

There are two important tests that you can use to determine if you are in good enough shape to handle the rigorous requirements of playing a game of full-court basketball. If you can pass these tests, you are in good enough shape to play basketball at a high level.

Not only are these tests, but they can also be used as a training method to increase your conditioning. By simply attempting to do the tests, you will improve your endurance and conditioning.

Test 1: Kansas City Basketball Conditioning Test

Step 1: Line up on the baseline.

Step 2: Sprint back and forth between the starting and opposite baselines twice, then stop at the free throw line. Finish entire sprint within 22 seconds.

Step 3: Rest 22 seconds.

Step 4: Perform a total of 20 reps.

If you can **complete this test,** you are on par with some of the top NCAA and NBA players in the world. This is an extremely difficult test, and you should be very proud of yourself if you can accomplish it. If you cannot finish the reps in 22 seconds or less, then do them as quickly as you can and finish out the full 20 reps.

Test 2: 1 Mile Run

For this test, you simply run one mile as quickly as you can and time yourself. Every time you do the test, try to get a quicker time. Below is a time reference to determine how well you are performing.

10 Minutes or above – You are out of shape and need to run more.

8-9 Minutes – You are in good enough shape to play a game of basketball, but not at a very high level or for a long time.

7-8 Minutes – You are in good basketball shape. Not elite, but good enough to play hard for a while.

6-7 Minutes – You are in great basketball shape. You can play hard and for a long time.

5-6 Minutes – You are in top NBA basketball shape. You are most likely in better shape than anyone you play against. Rip Hamilton, NBA player known for being in great shape, can complete the run in roughly 5 minutes.

Under 5 Minutes – You should be a runner! You are in phenomenal shape.

Recovery and Injury Prevention

Static and dynamic stretches are extremely important when it comes to preventing injuries and recovering.

Static Stretching

Static stretching typically occurs after your workout and during off days. To perform a static stretch, keep the body at rest while staying in one position as you stretch the muscle or muscles. One example is sitting on the floor, bringing the bottoms of your feet together, and leaning forward from the hips. Stay in that position for several seconds.

Dynamic Stretching

Dynamic stretching typically occurs before a workout to warm up the muscles. This style of stretching uses the momentum of an isolated movement to stretch a muscle. For example, the lunge stretch, taking a large step, planting your foot, then bending the knee and holding it above your planted foot, while keeping your torso straight, is considered a dynamic stretch.

NOTE: Specific stretches will be explained in the ***Drills and Exercises*** segment.

Recovery and Injury Prevention

DRILLS AND EXERCISES

The drills and exercises are based off everything you just learned. They are separated into dribbling, passing, shooting, defense, athleticism, and recovery and injury prevention categories

1. ***RECOVERY AND INJURY PREVENTION – DYNAMIC WARMUP***

   These should be done before all basketball drills or weightlifting exercises.

   NOTE: When to do them is listed in the actual program drills.

   – **Stationary squats** 10 reps

– **Lunges** 10 reps per each leg

– **Side leg swings** 10 reps per each leg

– **Front leg swings** 10 reps per each leg

- **Toe touches** 10 reps

- **Power skipping down the court**

- **High knees down the court**

- **Butt kicks down the court**

- **Jog full court and back** 2 reps

- **Defensive slide half court and back**

  In the position on your left, you must run back and forth between the sides of the court as fast as possible. You can go from back line to free throw line or back line to center line. You must stay low throughout and tap the ground on each side.

- **60% sprint full court**

  Starting at the baseline, sprint 60% of the way down the court. Then slow down and stop before reaching the opposite baseline.

- **70% sprint full court**
- **80% sprint full court**
- **5 stationary jump and lands (75-80% effort)**

By the time you are done with this warm up, you should have broken a sweat and feel completely loose and ready to go.

2. *RECOVERY AND INJURY PREVENTION – STATIC STRETCHING*

This should be done after your workouts and on off days. It helps maintain/increase your flexibility and assists you in recovering fully for the next workouts. Get a timer and hold the stretches for the given amount of time. Don't cheat!

– **Hip stretch** 1 minute per hip

- **Sitting hamstring stretch** 1 minute

- **Sitting quad stretch** 2 minutes

- **Lying gluteus stretch** 1 minute per leg

– **Lower leg stretch** 1 minute

– **Side splits attempt** 30 seconds

– **Front splits attempt** 30 seconds per leg

3. *DRIBBLING – BALL HANDLING CIRCUIT*

This will drastically improve your dribbling skills. The entire circuit should be finished in 5-10 min. Make sure to do every exercise as quickly as possible, with your head up, and be in control. If you lose control of the ball, sometimes, that is good! It means you are pushing yourself.

Take a look at the "Ball Handling and Dribbling." chapter for a description of these kinds of dribbling.

Go through the whole chapter before you start your practice.

- **Finger taps and slaps** 30 seconds
  Tap and slap the basketball with your fingers for warm-up
- **Continuous circles around head, waist, legs**
  Do the circles with the ball around your head, waist, and legs, change direction after 5 reps
- **Control dribble waist** 20 reps
- **Control dribble above head** 20 reps
- **Power dribble** 20 reps
  Dribble between legs while walking or brisk walking. Increase your speed, change angles, practice with zigzag walking patterns or figure 8s. Put as much variation in your drill to increase efficacy.
- **Stationary crossovers alternating between long and close** 25 reps
  Dribble with one hand, and then switch to the other. Dribble the ball higher and then lower.
- **Stationary crossover between legs** 25 reps
  Do a crossover between your legs while standing. Change the legs.
- **Stationary dribbles behind the back** 25 reps
- **One hand pendulum dribbles forward** 20 reps per each hand
- **One hand pendulum dribbles backwards** 20 reps per each hand
- **Alternating pendulum dribbles forward/backwards/**

switching hands 10 reps
- **Rapid figure 8 dribbles forward** 5 reps
- **Rapid figure 8 dribbles backwards** 5 reps

4. *DRIBBLING* – BASIC 3 *DRIBBLING TRANSITION*

This works on the basic three dribbles and increases your ability to transition between them.

Speed dribble to half court, Control dribble to the 3-point line, Power dribble to the baseline. Walk back to the other side of the court. 5 reps

5. *DRIBBLING* – *DRIVE AND JAB FAKE DRIVES*

This works on your drive and jab fake drives.

You are going to drive both left and right from five total spots around the 3-point line.

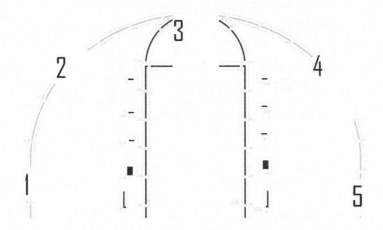

- Spin the ball to yourself, catch it, and put it into your triple threat position, then **drive right** and do a layup. Get your re- bound, go back to the same spot and **drive left** and do a layup. Once you go both left and right from a single spot, move onto the next spot. You are finished when you have done a *total of 10 reps.*

– Catch your breath, then repeat the exact same thing, however, this time, do **jab fake drives** instead.

6. *DRIBBLING – CROSSOVER CIRCUIT*

This works on your crossovers. Make sure to try to move the ball as quickly as you can and keep your head up. You will take a few dribbles, do a crossover, then take a few more dribbles and do another crossover, and keep going the entire length of the court. Do 2 reps of each exercise.

Take a look at the "Ball Handling and Dribbling." chapter for a description of these kinds of dribbling.

Go through the whole chapter again before you start your practice.

– **Full court & back regular crossovers**
– **Full court & back between legs crossovers**
– **Full court & back behind the back crossovers**
– **Full court & back spin crossovers**
– **Full court & back in and out crossovers**
– **Full court & back double crossovers (any combination you want)**
– **Full court & back triple crossovers (any combination you want)**

7. *SHOOTING – POST SKILLS CIRCUIT*

This drill will help you finish around the rim. The objective is to make as many lay-ups as possible. Do, at least, 25 reps for each of these drills.

– **Mikan drill**

  • Standing inside the block, to one side of the basket, face the baseline. Jump and shoot a lay-up. Use the backboard for each attempt.
  • Once you land, rebound the ball. Aim for when the ball is at the highest point. Keep the ball above your head when you grab it.

- Jumping should put you on the other side of the basket.

- Jump and attempt another lay-up without stopping.

- Continue alternating lay-ups from the right side to the left side.

- Explode toward the basket by jumping off one leg for each shot.

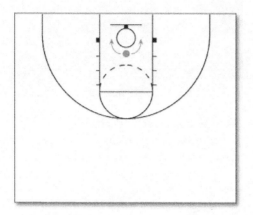

- **Reverse Mikan drill**
  Execute Mikan drill by performing reverse lay-up with your back to the baseline.

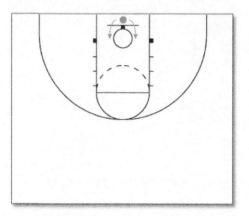

- **Two ball Mikan drill**
  Perform Mikan drill holding two balls in your hands.

– **Two ball reverse Mikan drill**
Execute two ball Mikan drill by performing a reverse lay-up with your back to the baseline.

8. *SHOOTING – STATIONARY FORM SHOOTING*

Focus on the basketball shooting technique that was taught earlier.

– **Straight on shots**

Go right up to the net and shoot 10 shots straight on.

— **Shot from the left**

Step left from the rim and take 10 shots.

— **Shot from the right**

Step right from the rim and take 10 shots.

9. *SHOOTING – HALF COURT TO FREE THROW JUMP SHOTS*

Pull up jump shot from free throw line
Dribble from half court to the free throw line and shoot a pull-up jump shot. Do 20 reps.

10. *SHOOTING – 1-2-3 FIVE BLOCK CIRCUIT*

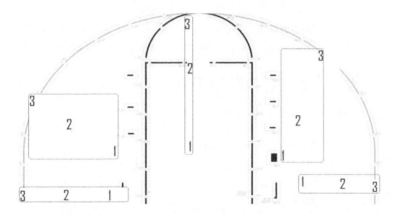

This drill will be shot in five different blocks. Once you are done with one block, you go to the next one without taking any breaks.

— Pick any block and start at point 1. Shoot a **regular set shot.** Keep shooting until you make three in a row.

— You then go to point 2 and shoot **pull-up jump shots.** Don't stop until you make three in a row.

— You then go to point 3 and shoot **regular 3 point shots.** You don't stop until you make 3 in a row.

— Once you have completed a block, you move to the next block.

Finish *all 5 blocks.*

11. SHOOTING – SHOOT 25 FREE THROWS

Don't forget about the lessons learned from Michael Jordan on the free throw shooting.

12. DEFENSE – DEFENSIVE CIRCUIT

Take a look at the "Defense." chapter for a description of defensive slides.

Go through the whole chapter before you start your practice. Do two reps of each of these drills:

- **Defensive slide from baseline to baseline**
  Go through the whole chapter before you start your practice. Do two reps of each of these drills:
- **Defensive slide zig-zag the entire length of the court**
  Pivot and change directions every time you do five slides

13. PASSING – PASSING CIRCUIT

Find a wall and make a target on it.

- **Chess passes against the wall**
  Do 25 chest passes against the wall, progressively moving farther out. Go as far as you can until you can't hit the target anymore.
- **Bounce passes against the wall**
  Do 25 bounce passes against the wall and progressively move farther out until you can't hit the target anymore.
- **Overhead passes against the wall**
  Do 25 overhead passes against the wall and progressively move farther out until you can't hit the target anymore.

14. CONDITIONING – 1 MILE RUN

Make sure you time yourself.

Check your results against the *Test 2* described in the "Conditioning." chapter.

15. CONDITIONING – KANSAS CITY BASKETBALL CON-DITIONING TEST

Step 1:   Line up on the baseline.

Step 2:   Sprint back and forth between the starting and opposite baselines twice, then stop at the free throw line. Finish entire sprint within 22 seconds.

Step 3:   Rest 22 seconds.

Step 4:   *Perform a total of 20 reps.*

Read more on "*Conditioning*" section.

16. ATHLETECISM – FULL OLYMPIC BACK SQUAT

Make sure you add weight to this every week. Do 3 sets of 6 reps.

17. ATHLETECISM – FRONT SQUAT

Make sure you add weight to this every week. Do 4 sets of 4 reps.

18. ATHLETECISM – BENCH PRESS

Make sure you add weight to this every week. Do 3 sets of 5 reps.

19. ATHLETECISM – PULL UP/CHIN UP CIRCUIT

Do the maximum number of pull-ups that you can do. Take a two-minute break, and then do the maximum number of chin-ups that you can do.

20. ATHLETECISM – BARBELL ROW

Make sure you add weight to this every week. Do 3 sets of 5 reps.

21. ATHLETECISM – MILITARY PRESS

For this exercise, you lift the bar over your head. Make sure you add weight to this every week. Do 3 sets of 5 reps.

22. ATHLETECISM – MAX EFFORT JUMP

Take 3 steps and jump as high as you can. Do 5 reps.

23. ATHLETECISM – MAX EFFORT STATIONARY JUMPS

Stand still and jump as high as you can. Do 5 reps.

THE 21-DAY PROGRAM

This program will use drills and exercises that will specifically increase your dribbling, passing, shooting, conditioning, and athleticism. *Each number in the program is coordinated with the same number under the "Drills and Exercises." section*. Therefore, in order to understand what to do for each exercise or drill, find and match the numbers for each day with the same number under the "Drills and Exercises." category.

You may want to make a copy of "The 21-Day Program" and cross off each exercise after you have completed it.

If, at any point, you feel completely beaten up, exhausted, and don't feel like working out, take the day off. You are overworked and need to recover!

If you try your best but can't add any weight to your exercises every week because it is too heavy, eat more food! Getting enough protein, carbohydrates, and healthy fats are essential to recovering. This is an intense session, so you must take good care of your body with good nutrition. You know you are eating enough if you feel energized and are able to gain strength every week. Also, when you practice, keep a bottle of electrolytes nearby, such as Gatorade or Tang.

No number of drills can be compared with a competitive game to test and develop team coordination and passing skills. *You must play, at least, two complete games every week*.

Have fun and good luck improving your basketball game!

DAY 1:

a) Drill #1 <u>Dynamic Warm Up</u>
b) Drill #22 <u>Max Effort Jump</u>
c) Drill #16 <u>Full Olympic Back Squat</u>
d) Drill #3 <u>Ball Handling Circuit</u>
e) Drill #4 <u>Basic 3 Dribbling Transition</u>
f) Drill #5 <u>Drive and Jab Fake Drives</u>
g) Drill #6 <u>Crossover Circuit</u>
h) Drill #7 <u>Post Skills Circuit</u>
i) Drill #8 <u>Stationary Form Shooting</u>
j) Drill #9 <u>Half Court to Free Throw Jump Shots</u>
k) Drill #10 <u>1-2-3 Five Block Circuit</u>
l) Drill #11 <u>Shoot 25 Free Throws</u>
m) Drill #12 <u>Defensive Circuit</u>
n) Drill #13 <u>Passing Circuit</u>
o) Drill #2 <u>Static Stretching</u>

DAY 2:

a) Drill #1 <u>Dynamic Warm Up</u>
b) Drill #18 <u>Bench Press</u>
c) Drill #19 <u>Pull Up/Chin Up Circuit</u>
d) Drill #20 <u>Barbell Row</u>
e) Drill #21 <u>Military Press</u>
f) Drill #3 <u>Ball Handling Circuit</u>
g) Drill #4 <u>Basic 3 Dribbling Transition</u>
h) Drill #5 <u>Drive and Jab Fake Drives</u>
i) Drill #6 <u>Crossover Circuit</u>
j) Drill #7 <u>Post Skills Circuit</u>
k) Drill #8 <u>Stationary Form Shooting</u>
l) Drill #9 <u>Half Court to Free Throw Jump Shots</u>
m) Drill #10 <u>1-2-3 Five Block Circuit</u>
n) Drill #11 <u>Shoot 25 Free Throws</u>
o) Drill #12 <u>Defensive Circuit</u>

p) Drill #13 <u>Passing Circuit</u>

q) Drill #2 <u>Static Stretching</u>

DAY 3:

a) Drill #1 <u>Dynamic Warm Up</u>

b) Drill #15 <u>Kansas City Basketball Conditioning Test</u>

c) Drill #3 <u>Ball Handling Circuit</u>

d) Drill #4 <u>Basic 3 Dribbling Transition</u>

e) Drill #5 <u>Drive and Jab Fake Drives</u>

f) Drill #6 <u>Crossover Circuit</u>

g) Drill #7 <u>Post Skills Circuit</u>

h) Drill #8 <u>Stationary Form Shooting</u>

i) Drill #9 <u>Half Court to Free Throw Jump Shots</u>

j) Drill #10 <u>1-2-3 Five Block Circuit</u>

k) Drill #11 <u>Shoot 25 Free Throws</u>

l) Drill #12 <u>Defensive Circuit</u>

m) Drill #13 <u>Passing Circuit</u>

n) Drill #2 <u>Static Stretching</u>

DAY 4:

a) Drill #1 <u>Dynamic Warm Up</u>

b) Drill #14 <u>1 Mile Run</u>

c) Drill #2 <u>Static Stretching</u>

DAY 5:

a) Drill #1 <u>Dynamic Warm Up</u>

b) Drill #23 <u>Max Effort Stationary Jumps</u>

c) Drill #3 <u>Ball Handling Circuit</u>

d) Drill #4 <u>Basic 3 Dribbling Transition</u>

e) Drill #5 <u>Drive and Jab Fake Drives</u>

f) Drill #6 <u>Crossover Circuit</u>

g) Drill #7 Post Skills Circuit
h) Drill #8 Stationary Form Shooting
i) Drill #9 Half Court to Free Throw Jump Shots
j) Drill #10 1-2-3 Five Block Circuit
k) Drill #11 Shoot 25 Free Throws
l) Drill #12 Defensive Circuit
m) Drill #13 Passing Circuit
n) Drill #2 Static Stretching

DAY 6:

a) Drill #2 Static Stretching

DAY 7:

Off day.

DAY 8:

a) Drill #1 Dynamic Warm Up
b) Drill #22 Max Effort Jump
c) Drill #16 Full Olympic Back Squat
d) Drill #3 Ball Handling Circuit
e) Drill #4 Basic 3 Dribbling Transition
f) Drill #5 Drive and Jab Fake Drives
g) Drill #6 Crossover Circuit
h) Drill #7 Post Skills Circuit
i) Drill #8 Stationary Form Shooting
j) Drill #9 Half Court to Free Throw Jump Shots
k) Drill #10 1-2-3 Five Block Circuit
l) Drill #11 Shoot 25 Free Throws
m) Drill #12 Defensive Circuit
n) Drill #13 Passing Circuit
o) Drill #2 Static Stretching

DAY 9:

a) Drill #1 <u>Dynamic Warm Up</u>

b) Drill #18 <u>Bench Press</u>

c) Drill #19 <u>Pull Up/Chin Up Circuit</u>

d) Drill #20 <u>Barbell Row</u>

e) Drill #21 <u>Military Press</u>

f) Drill #3 <u>Ball Handling Circuit</u>

g) Drill #4 <u>Basic 3 Dribbling Transition</u>

h) Drill #5 <u>Drive and Jab Fake Drives</u>

i) Drill #6 <u>Crossover Circuit</u>

j) Drill #7 <u>Post Skills Circuit</u>

k) Drill #8 <u>Stationary Form Shooting</u>

l) Drill #9 <u>Half Court to Free Throw Jump Shots</u>

m) Drill #10 <u>1-2-3 Five Block Circuit</u>

n) Drill #11 <u>Shoot 25 Free Throws</u>

o) Drill #12 <u>Defensive Circuit</u>

p) Drill #13 <u>Passing Circuit</u>

q) Drill #2 <u>Static Stretching</u>

DAY 10:

a) Drill #1 <u>Dynamic Warm Up</u>

b) Drill #15 <u>Kansas City Basketball Conditioning Test</u>

c) Drill #3 <u>Ball Handling Circuit</u>

d) Drill #4 <u>Basic 3 Dribbling Transition</u>

e) Drill #5 <u>Drive and Jab Fake Drives</u>

f) Drill #6 <u>Crossover Circuit</u>

g) Drill #7 <u>Post Skills Circuit</u>

h) Drill #8 <u>Stationary Form Shooting</u>

i) Drill #9 <u>Half Court to Free Throw Jump Shots</u>

j) Drill #10 <u>1-2-3 Five Block Circuit</u>

k) Drill #11 <u>Shoot 25 Free Throws</u>

l) Drill #12 <u>Defensive Circuit</u>

m) Drill #13 <u>Passing Circuit</u>

n)   Drill #2 <u>Static Stretching</u>

DAY 11:

a)   Drill #1 <u>Dynamic Warm Up</u>
b)   Drill #14 <u>1 Mile Run</u>
c)   Drill #2 <u>Static Stretching</u>

DAY 12:

a)   Drill #1 <u>Dynamic Warm Up</u>
b)   Drill #23 <u>Max Effort Stationary Jumps</u>
c)   Drill #3 <u>Ball Handling Circuit</u>
d)   Drill #4 <u>Basic 3 Dribbling Transition</u>
e)   Drill #5 <u>Drive and Jab Fake Drives</u>
f)   Drill #6 <u>Crossover Circuit</u>
g)   Drill #7 <u>Post Skills Circuit</u>
h)   Drill #8 <u>Stationary Form Shooting</u>
i)   Drill #9 <u>Half Court to Free Throw Jump Shots</u>
j)   Drill #10 <u>1-2-3 Five Block Circuit</u>
k)   Drill #11 <u>Shoot 25 Free Throws</u>
l)   Drill #12 <u>Defensive Circuit</u>
m)   Drill #13 <u>Passing Circuit</u>
n)   Drill #2 <u>Static Stretching</u>

DAY 13:

a)   Drill #2 <u>Static Stretching</u>

DAY 14:

Off day.

DAY 15:

a) Drill #1 <u>Dynamic Warm Up</u>

b) Drill #22 <u>Max Effort Jump</u>

c) Drill #16 <u>Full Olympic Back Squat</u>

d) Drill #3 <u>Ball Handling Circuit</u>

e) Drill #4 <u>Basic 3 Dribbling Transition</u>

f) Drill #5 <u>Drive and Jab Fake Drives</u>

g) Drill #6 <u>Crossover Circuit</u>

h) Drill #7 <u>Post Skills Circuit</u>

i) Drill #8 <u>Stationary Form Shooting</u>

j) Drill #9 <u>Half Court to Free Throw Jump Shots</u>

k) Drill #10 <u>1-2-3 Five Block Circuit</u>

l) Drill #11 <u>Shoot 25 Free Throws</u>

m) Drill #12 <u>Defensive Circuit</u>

n) Drill #13 <u>Passing Circuit</u>

o) Drill #2 <u>Static Stretching</u>

DAY 16:

a) Drill #1 <u>Dynamic Warm Up</u>

b) Drill #18 <u>Bench Press</u>

c) Drill #19 <u>Pull Up/Chin Up Circuit</u>

d) Drill #20 <u>Barbell Row</u>

e) Drill #21 <u>Military Press</u>

f) Drill #3 <u>Ball Handling Circuit</u>

g) Drill #4 <u>Basic 3 Dribbling Transition</u>

h) Drill #5 <u>Drive and Jab Fake Drives</u>

i) Drill #6 <u>Crossover Circuit</u>

j) Drill #7 <u>Post Skills Circuit</u>

k) Drill #8 <u>Stationary Form Shooting</u>

l) Drill #9 <u>Half Court to Free Throw Jump Shots</u>

m) Drill #10 <u>1-2-3 Five Block Circuit</u>

n) Drill #11 <u>Shoot 25 Free Throws</u>

o) Drill #12 <u>Defensive Circuit</u>

p) Drill #13 <u>Passing Circuit</u>
q) Drill #2 <u>Static Stretching</u>

DAY 17:

a) Drill #1 <u>Dynamic Warm Up</u>
b) Drill #15 <u>Kansas City Basketball Conditioning Test</u>
c) Drill #3 <u>Ball Handling Circuit</u>
d) Drill #4 <u>Basic 3 Dribbling Transition</u>
e) Drill #5 <u>Drive and Jab Fake Drives</u>
f) Drill #6 <u>Crossover Circuit</u>
g) Drill #7 <u>Post Skills Circuit</u>
h) Drill #8 <u>Stationary Form Shooting</u>
i) Drill #9 <u>Half Court to Free Throw Jump Shots</u>
j) Drill #10 <u>1-2-3 Five Block Circuit</u>
k) Drill #11 <u>Shoot 25 Free Throws</u>
l) Drill #12 <u>Defensive Circuit</u>
m) Drill #13 <u>Passing Circuit</u>
n) Drill #2 <u>Static Stretching</u>

DAY 18:

a) Drill #1 <u>Dynamic Warm Up</u>
b) Drill #14 <u>1 Mile Run</u>
c) Drill #2 <u>Static Stretching</u>

DAY 19:

a) Drill #1 <u>Dynamic Warm Up</u>
b) Drill #23 <u>Max Effort Stationary Jumps</u>
c) Drill #3 <u>Ball Handling Circuit</u>
d) Drill #4 <u>Basic 3 Dribbling Transition</u>
e) Drill #5 <u>Drive and Jab Fake Drives</u>
f) Drill #6 <u>Crossover Circuit</u>

g) Drill #7 <u>Post Skills Circuit</u>
h) Drill #8 <u>Stationary Form Shooting</u>
i) Drill #9 <u>Half Court to Free Throw Jump Shots</u>
j) Drill #10 <u>1-2-3 Five Block Circuit</u>
k) Drill #11 <u>Shoot 25 Free Throws</u>
l) Drill #12 <u>Defensive Circuit</u>
m) Drill #13 <u>Passing Circuit</u>
n) Drill #2 <u>Static Stretching</u>

DAY 20:

a) Drill #2 <u>Static Stretching</u>

DAY 21:

Off day.

CONCLUSION

Congratulations! You have finished the program by working hard in the past 21 days.

You have learned how to improve your shooting, dribbling, passing, defense, athleticism, conditioning, how to prevent injuries, and how to recover. Not only did you learn how to do this, but you have actually gone out and done it! I am sure that by this stage your practice sessions have moved beyond one-on-one practices to actual friendly games.

If you want to continue to see improvements, you could do the program a second time through. Simply start at Day 1 again!

Let's recap some major lessons learned throughout this book, and what better way to do that than through the teachings of basketball legends.

Important Lessons from Basketball Legends

- John Wooden won 10 NCAA championships coaching at UCLA. He taught players such as Kareem Abdul-Jabbar and Bill Walton. Twenty-four of his players made it to All American. John always stressed that *every player should be in peak condition*. Teach them the value of the game and the fundamentals. Hit the open man on offense and drill the values of team play. Defense is hard work and takes time to build, but the offense should not be solely responsible for winning.

- Kareem Abdul-Jabbar said about Coach Wooden: "The biggest lesson I learned from him was *preparation*." Kareem went on to become the leading all-time scorer in NBA with 38387 points! He followed the advice through and through by training with coaches as diverse as Bruce Lee.

- Magic Johnson, a retired American basketball player, is designated one of the 50 Greatest NBA Players in History. He was a member of the Dream Team, played for the Lakers, and was rated by ESPN as the greatest NBA point guard of all time in 2007. The legend had to undergo major struggles in his life due to HIV. However, he dedicated his life to increasing AIDS awareness and philanthropy. His message is simple— *tolerance for each other*.

- And lastly, we have Michael Jordan, designated by ESPN as the greatest North American athlete of the twentieth century. The Associated Press listed him second, after Babe Ruth, among their list of notable athletes from that century. His biggest message to us all is that "*in life, you get what you expect and accept. If you answer these questions you will change your life.*"

Prep Talk

Whatever the nature or type of sport, be it baseball, football, basketball etc., nothing motivates a team better than a strong coach; one who has principles is able to draw the performance out of you and knows the right thing to say at the right time.

A seasoned basketball team in the locker room, about to step out on the court, might feel confident. However, an excellent prep talk can mean the difference between a good performance and an extraordinary game. Although there are many types of prep talks your coach can give you, since this is your own program, we want you to take the reins and visualize…

- Tell yourself how hard you have been practicing for the past 21 days.
- Tell yourself about the time dedicated and the sacrifices you made. Think about what this game means to you.
- Also think about the opponent, how it has lost or won against you? What are their weaknesses?
- Now visualize. Close your eyes and take nice deep breaths while imagining the game.
- Imagine yourself rushing out of the locker room, and as you hit the court, the crowd erupts in a chorus.
- You can sense the smell of the court and the temperature on your skin. Yes, you are at the right place, and you are very comfortable on the court because you spend most of your time here at practice and other games. This is your territory, and the opponent does not have a chance.
- Now, imagine the sound of the referee's whistle, the ball is tossed in the air, and your offense jumps and gets possession of the ball. The opponent does not stand a chance.
- Repeatedly, you shoot, dunk, and dodge the ball in the basket.
- You smile at the opponents. You respect them, but you are here to win, and you repeatedly make the basket and block their shots if they shoot any.
- You steamroll over them!

Now that you are trained, focused, and prepared, it's time to rock and roll! Play to win!

ABOUT THE AUTHOR

James Wilson is a certified personal trainer and professional basketball coach. He has been developing young basketball players to excel in their game for over 30 years. He has worked with coaches and basketball players in more than 20 countries worldwide, which has enabled him to develop a unique playing style and coaching method.

His coaching philosophy revolves around three fundamental concepts: best possible player conditioning, quickness, and conviction. These key points should be followed in every aspect of the game, but when they are followed in every aspect of life, a basketball player can become truly great.

There are thousands of drills that can be practiced to improve your basketball game. Even NBA players cannot pinpoint the exact programs that should be selected or discarded. However, with experience, seasoned coaches can give a guideline of drills most useful at the start of a new season. Thus, this book can be looked at as a summation of the most important lessons the author has meticulously taught his students for over 30 years of his life.

Made in United States
North Haven, CT
11 July 2024

54649543R00054